Roger Clemens

ROCKET!

by
Kevin Kernan

SPORTS PUBLISHING INC.
www.SportsPublishingInc.com

Production manager: Susan M. McKinney
Cover design: Scot Muncaster
Photos: *The Associated Press*, University of Texas

ISBN: 1-58261-128-9
Library of Congress Catalog Card Number: 99-64417

SPORTS PUBLISHING INC.
SportsPublishingInc.com

Printed in the United States.

CONTENTS

Roger pitched in the Yankees' first game of the 1999 season. (AP/Wide World Photos)

CHAPTER ONE

Growing Up Fast

The little boy was scared. He knew something was terribly wrong. His stepfather staggered away from the kitchen table, pain tearing through his chest. The ambulance had come to the house in Dayton, Ohio, and the boy was ushered to the basement by his older sister to keep him away from the upsetting scene.

At nine years old, this was the only father the boy knew. Woody Booher, a tool and die maker, had lovingly treated the boy like his own son. The child's own dad left the family when the boy was only 3 1/2 months old. As difficult as it was, the little boy had to see what was going on, so he piled a stack of books under a basement window, climbed his unsteady tower and looked out. "It was his second heart attack," the boy recalled years later, "but this time I knew it was bad."

What he saw tore at his own heart. His stepfather, who had been so wonderful to the boy and his five brothers and sisters, was being carried away. The boy would never forget the pain of that night even though he would grow up to be 6'4", 225 pounds and become baseball's Rocket Man.

Roger Clemens is the most dominant pitcher of his era, the first pitcher to ever win five Cy Young Awards, the annual award presented to the American and National League's top pitcher. Twice he was the unanimous winner of the Cy Young Award Roger also won the Most Valuable Player Award in 1986, baseball's most coveted award. He throws a baseball 96 mph with pinpoint control. That's how he became The Rocket.

That night when he was nine, though, has never left him, and the loss of his father and stepfather helped shape the dominating pitcher he became. The right-hander has the work ethic of a coal miner, the determination of a long-distance runner and the skill of a surgeon. Roger, as baseball scouts love to say, is the complete pitching package, a pitching machine.

That night also made him determined to be there for his own four sons. "I've missed my dad every day since," he would say years later. "I can't tell you how painful it was for me . . . . When I see my teammates in the clubhouse hugging their fathers, I think, 'You're taking this for granted.' It's not resentment or jealousy; it's just wishful thinking on my part.

Roger raises the Texas Longhorns symbols during ceremonies retiring his University of Texas jersey. (University of Texas)

"I can't ever remember wanting for anything except possibly a father in the stands watching me pitch," he said in his autobiography, *Rocket Man*.

Roger has never taken life for granted. He is not afraid to make a change if he thinks it is best for him and his family. His first 12 years in the majors were with the Boston Red Sox. He was their trademark player and he carried them to the World Series in 1986, before losing in heartbreaking fashion to the Mets.

Roger never looked back, however, when he joined the Toronto Blue Jays as a free agent in 1997. At the time, his critics in Boston thought he was done, on the downside of a brilliant career at the age of 34 because he had posted a 10-13 record in 1996 and was only one game over .500 (40-39) the previous four seasons combined. He had not won 20 games in a season since 1990.

Roger tries on his new cap while manager Joe Torre holds his new jersey. (AP/Wide World Photos)

He walked away as a free agent, not only leaving Boston, but leaving the country, too, signing a staggering $31.1 million, four-year contract with the Toronto Blue Jays in December of 1996, hoping he had moved closer to a championship.

Though Roger went on to win two more Cy Young awards in Toronto, producing an amazing 41-13 record in the process, he never got his championship ring.

No matter how difficult a decision, Roger knew he must move on again. Like the nine-year-old child stacking those books together to peer out the window, he knew what he had to do. He was able to work out a trade to the World Champion Yankees just before the start of the 1999 spring training, a deal that sent Yankee ace David Wells, young second baseman Homer Bush and reliever Graeme Lloyd to Toronto. Though Wells was loved in New York because of his excellent pitching—he fired a perfect game in 1998 and his eccentric ways; he once went to the mound wearing Babe Ruth's cap— it was a trade the Yankees could not turn down. The best pitcher in baseball now belonged to the best team in baseball. This was the perfect baseball marriage.

The Yanks won 125 games in 1998, but every other team was gearing up to beat them. "No one could come up with a reason not to make the deal," the Yankees 31-year-old general manager Brian Cashman said when the trade was made on Feb. 18, 1999. "He's not just a pitcher. He's an animal. And he's our animal now."

Veteran right-hander David Cone, one of the most popular Yankees said, "If they'd have thrown me in, it still would have been a great deal."

Two days after the trade was made, Clemens reported to team's spring training site in Tampa, Florida. The name of the stadium is only fitting Legends Field. Another legend had been added to the Yankees roster.

In 1986, Roger set the major league record for
strikeouts in a game (20). (AP/Wide World Photos)

2

A Night To Remember

Athletes love to talk about being in The Zone, where all is perfect in their world as they effortlessly reach their peak performance.

There are only a handful of times when such perfection is achieved on the major league level. One of those times came the night of April 29, 1986. That night, in only his second year in the majors, Roger struck out 20 Seattle Mariners in a nine-inning game in Fenway Park in Boston. His final strikeout came against Phil Bradley in the ninth. That gave Roger more strikeouts in one game than by any pitcher in 111 years. He also tied the American League record with eight straight strikeouts in that game.

There are only 27 outs in a nine-inning baseball game. To get 20 on strikeouts at the major league level is incredible. It was as if Roger were back in Little League. It was there as a nine-year-old where his gift was first recognized. "He struck out the side on nine pitches," his mother Bess Wright remembered, years later, "and the catcher's glove made a popping noise. That's when I thought we had something special in the family."

There was something special that night against the Mariners when Roger broke a record that was held by four pitchers, including his idol, fellow Texan Nolan Ryan, in the 3-1 win. "Unbelievable," Roger said after the game. The next day he couldn't believe it, either. "It just didn't sink in, what it all meant," he said. "But my teammates were all ex-

Roger's record-setting 1986 performance came only eight months after shoulder surgery. (AP/Wide World Photos)

cited and when I got home I got calls from a lot of my family. Most of them live in Houston. And my brothers were crying, and my mother was crying and they said, "You're in the Hall of Fame."

Those magical nine innings set the tone for the season. Roger's performance came only eight months after shoulder surgery. The Red Sox manager at the time was John McNamara. "I've never seen a pitching performance as awesome as that, and I don't think you will again in the history of baseball," he said after the game. Little did he know that Roger would again accomplish the feat 10 years later.

Roger's teammate Bruce Hurst had spent 11 years in the organization and saw a transformation during that game. The Red Sox had the superstar pitcher that would make the difference. "After that night," Hurst recalled years later, "we knew we were going to win the pennant."

They couldn't lose because Roger couldn't lose. He won 14 straight that season before taking his first loss. Winning is what Roger is all about. His hero is John F. Kennedy even though Roger was only one when the president was assassinated. One of Roger's favorite sayings is: "If you're not getting better, you're getting worse." It took nine years in the majors before Roger posted his first losing season, an 11-14 mark in 1993.

In the shorthand world of keeping score in baseball, a strikeout is recorded as a K. Now you know why the letter K is so important to Roger and why the name of his four boys all start with K. There is Koby (12), Kory (11), Kacy (5) and Kody (3). Koby was to be born eight months after Roger struck out 20.

His wife Debbie says that Roger is always ready to pitch, sometimes too ready.

"Sometimes he takes baseball too seriously," she told the *Boston Globe* in 1990. "The day he plays, he's a bear. He's got his game face on. He looks like a grizzly. I tell him that getting to the field two hours before a game is enough time to concentrate. I tell him: help your nerves! Thinking of nothing but the game all day is too long. One day we played tennis before the game. That was the day that he struck out 20 people. He was relaxed. So I said to Roger: 'See.'"

Roger went on to win 24 games that season and only lose four for the American League Champion Red Sox and was a unanimous choice for the Cy Young Award and the league's MVP. The 24 wins were the most by a Red Sox pitcher in 37 years. That year the Red Sox came within one strike of winning the World Championship but were beaten by the Mets in one of baseball's all-time great comebacks. One win away from winning the Series,

Ten years after his first 20-strikeout performance, Roger repeated the feat against the Detroit Tigers. (AP/ Wide World Photos)

Roger started Game 6 and left in the eighth inning with a 3-2 lead. The Mets went on to tie the game and then trailing by two, scored three times in the bottom of the 10th to pull out the victory. The Series was tied and the Mets won the seventh game, as Roger never got the chance to pitch in the final game. To this day he yearns for another chance to win a championship and pitch in the season's final game.

Ten years after his 20-strikeout performance on another brisk night, September 18th in Tiger Stadium, Clemens made the old ballpark young again by striking out 20 Tigers, tying his own major league record, a mark that the Cubs' Kerry Wood also tied in 1998. That night Roger went into that game trying to tie legendary pitcher Cy Young's career Red Sox' records of 38 shutouts and 192 victories. He not only caught Young, he caught up with his own legend by using a fastball that was

Roger and the Longhorns won the NCAA championship in 1983. (Mike Forcucci, University of Texas)

clocked at 96 mph in the ninth inning, striking out the final batter of the night, Travis Fryman, to duplicate his amazing feat.

"It's incredible," Roger said that night. "I mentioned (Young's record) to a few guys before the game because it's important to me. I'm just very thankful I was able to do something I did 10 years ago." Back then he was a boyish 23-year-old out of the University of Texas. On this night he was a man, the father of four. His family watched him match his own record back home in Texas after coming home from his oldest son Koby's football game. He said Koby told him, " 'Dad, did you upstage me?'"

What he really did was upstage himself. Even Cy Young would have to tip his hat over that deed. Roger was a strong at the end of the game, as he was at the beginning. "When you're chasing the guy they named the pitching awards after, boy, you don't get tired," Roger said.

Roger works hard to be the best pitcher he can be. (AP/ Wide World Photos)

Tiger shortstop Allan Trammell, a great player in his own right, put it all in perspective when he said, "Roger knows what he's doing. He doesn't just rear back and throw. That's why he's Roger Clemens, destined for greatness ... already great."

CHAPTER THREE

His Mother's Pride

Roger prides himself on hard work. He labors endlessly to perfect his mechanics, working to get his legs in top condition to become the pitcher he is today. A great pitcher is a combination of God-given talent and hard work. Not just working in the weight room and on the field, but working to mentally discipline himself. The hours thinking about his pitches and his approach to the hitters. Every pitch has a purpose. Roger never just throws the ball, he is always in there pitching.

Roger as a senior in high school. (Spring Woods High School)

Roger played football, baseball and basketball in high school. (Spring Woods High School)

Growing up, that work ethic was instilled by his mother, Bessie Jane and his grandmother Myrtle Lee. His brother Randy, who is 10 years older than Roger, watched out for him as Roger grew up. There were six children in the family and Roger said early in his career that his mom and grandmother, "Taught me values. They gave me discipline and they gave me great direction."

Once his stepfather passed away, it was up to his mother to become the breadwinner of the family and she worked long hours. "I watched her stock coolers, clean buildings, work all day and night to make sure her kids had a good life," Roger once told *Sports Illustrated*. "We were probably lower class growing up, but no one knew it. I always had the best spikes, the best gloves. People thought we had money."

His mom and grandmother also gave him the support any child, any athlete needs. When he

Roger with the Spring Woods High School baseball team his senior year. (Spring Woods High School)

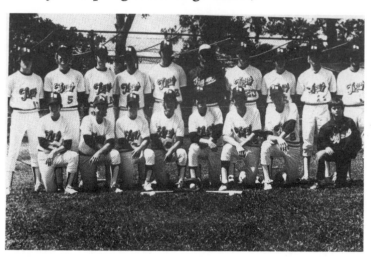

needed to talk something out, they were there for him. "I rely a lot on my mother and grandmother," he said, after he became a star with the Red Sox. "When push comes to shove, I call my mom and she'll give me three or four different versions and tell me, "Now, it's your decision.""

His choice, just like the pitches he selects when he attacks a batter.

A parent can point a child in the right direction, it's up to the child to learn the difference between right and wrong and the repercussions of those decisions. "With my mother working extra jobs, my grandmother raised me more than anybody," he once said. "She always said, 'I made you a man when you were a boy.'"

How did that great arm develop? With sunshine and love, thanks to grapes from his grandmother's vine. Roger, like any kid couldn't pass up such a temptation. He would pick the grapes and throw them at nearby targets. Later, a baseball would fit perfectly into that right hand and become Roger's missile of choice, thrown hard and with the same precision as those grapes.

Though he got in trouble with his grandmother for such pranks, Roger always tried to make the right decision and stand up for what he believes in even if it is not the most popular stance. With the Red Sox, he made the team improve conditions for the players' wives at the games, getting them better seats and a nice place for them to wait after games for their husbands.

Many people think that pitching came easy for Roger, but he worked hard for everything. "When I was coming up, no one said that I was a natural," he says. "They never said I was a can't-miss prospect. I didn't open everyone's eyes."

He said his ability was doubted and he used that as strength, something to light the fire inside his belly, instead of a crutch. When people said he couldn't do something, Roger became more determined to get the job done.

"I decided to prove them wrong," he says. "That's what got me to the big league level. That's what made me a power thrower."

He once said that even his relatives think that he simply walks on the field every fifth day and simply throws hard, but there is much more to his approach. "I go out to win," he says. "When I lose I make no excuses. I face up to one thing: I pitched badly."

His mom was always there for him. He said he never had to prove anything to her and even when he faltered as a youngster, she accepted those faults and strengthened his inner spirit to make him the pitcher and person that he is today.

Yankees manager Joe Torre watches Roger throw at Legends Field in Florida. (AP/Wide World Photos)

"I never had to prove myself to my Mom," he once told the *Boston Globe*. "As stubborn and as hardheaded as I've always been, she understands. When I was a kid, I wrecked her house. She'd have everyone over for dinner and I'd yank the cushions off the couch to mess things up. I played war with my sisters. Despite all that my mom always made me feel that I was someone special."

Every fifth day, he is a special pitcher. Every day he tries to be the best husband and father he can be.

Yankee catcher Joe Girardi calls Roger's approach on the field a winning attitude. "He brings a lot of emotion and he has great stuff," Girardi says. "But he has a will to win and you have to respect that. If you know Roger Clemens, he wants to win every day."

And that was one of the big reasons Roger came to the Yankees. They remind him of himself. "This team," he says proudly, "doesn't quit."

Koby Clemens sprays his dad with champagne after Roger's record fifth Cy Young Award in 1998. (AP/ Wide World Photos)

CHAPTER FOUR

Family Fun

He's known as Rocket Man, but he's really a Rocket Dad. Roger and his wife Debbie have four children. Call it his own little K-Korner. Kody is the youngest. There is also Kacy, Koby and Kory. In December of 1996, Roger decided to leave the Red Sox. Following a 13-year career with Boston, it was a difficult move to make. But he felt unappreciated by the Red Sox and, more importantly, he wanted to make sure his family felt at home with his new ball club. Roger deeply considers his family in his baseball decisions.

Roger felt that the Red Sox did not want his children around the ballpark. He thought a ballpark was the perfect place to bring his children and to work out with them hours before the game when they wouldn't bother the team.

Many ballplayers love to bring their children to work. It's no different than any dad showing his business to his sons. Considering how strongly Roger felt about baseball and his family, it was no surprise that when he decided to talk seriously to the Toronto Blue Jays about switching to their team as a free agent, the first question he asked Paul Beeston, who was then Blue Jays' president and CEO, was about his four children. Would they be welcomed in the Skydome? When Beeston visited Clemens in his Houston home in November of 1996, Roger asked, "What's the team's rule about kids on the field?" Family comes first with Roger and the Blue Jays made it clear that Roger and his children were always welcome to play any time they wanted at Skydome, provided, of course, it was not in the middle of a Blue Jays game. "I wanted to be able to come to the ballpark at two in the afternoon and hit ground balls to my kids."

Roger brings his family with him to his baseball home when the school year is over. Back home in Houston, Texas, Roger explained to *USA Today* what his typical family day was like in the off-season. He awakes at dawn to supervise the breakfast routine with Debbie. He then chauffeurs his oldest children off to school. By 8:15 in the morning he's in his upstairs gym for three hours of aerobics and weight training, taking extra care to strengthen his stomach and leg muscles.

A pitcher throws with his arm, but he wins with his legs—and abdominal muscles and Roger always takes care to work those areas extra hard. That is why he has had long-term success. In much the same

Roger signs autographs after his first Spring training game. (AP/Wide World Photos)

way, another Hall of Fame pitcher from Texas named Nolan Ryan followed the same type of routine.

As proud as Roger is of his family, his four children are just as proud of him.

"I'll be eating a bowl of cereal in my underwear, look up and see 11 kids standing in my kitchen," he told *USA Today*. "Koby will tell them, 'See, there he is. Roger Clemens, The Rocket. Wave, Dad, okay?' Then he'll say, 'All right, guys, can we go play ball now. I want to be Mo Vaughn, Kory, you're Mike Greenwell.'"

His kids may make believe they are Derek Jeter, Tino Martinez or Paul O'Neill now that Roger is a Yankee.

And Roger is like any other Little League father trying his best to help coach a team. Except Roger has all those strikeouts and wins and when he gives a pitching lesson, the kids really listen.

Roger sponsors and helps coach youth teams in the Houston area and is involved in every detail of putting a team together, including selecting the right batting helmets for his players. During his years in Boston he was extremely active in the Jimmy V Fund and cancer research for children. He would often drop in at hospitals wearing his Red Sox uniform to visit with sick children. Later, he started charity for children "K for Kids" program and is now involved in singer Garth Brooks' program for children, the "Touch 'Em All Foundation."

In baseball, a high fastball is referred to as chin music so it was only natural that Roger and Garth hook up. The famous country singer is a huge baseball fan and played for San Diego Padres in spring training of 1999. "He called and is trying to touch a lot of bases," Roger said of the foundation. "He's doing a lot of charitable things and we're going to get involved making contributions for each strikeout this year. I know he's really doing a lot of great things for various charities and we want to get involved.

"I think some people in baseball he knows turned him in my direction because they knew about my involvement with Ks for Kids last year," says Roger, who also admired Brooks' quest to get involved with baseball at the age of 37. "I do know he is taking it seriously, but what he's doing for charities is more serious."

When Garth got his first cherished spring training hit, he said something that Roger could relate to. "I wish my dad was here," Garth said.

Roger wants to be there for his children. He knows that baseball is more than a game, it's a labor of love that is passed down from one generation to the next. The lessons of the game are many. So often in today's world the wrong message is sent. The game has given Roger everything he's got, simply incredible riches, but at the same time, the re-

Roger wants to spend as much time with his family as he can. (AP/Wide World Photos)

lentless schedule and the time away from home tears at Roger's heart. He longs to spend as much time with his family as possible.

"There are four reasons why I'll probably retire sooner than I should, and they're right here at home" he says. "I work hard at being the best pitcher in baseball, but I work even harder at being a good father."

CHAPTER FIVE

A Kid at Heart

Roger is nonstop action, always talking, and he loves to play all kinds of games. He cherishes golf and his biggest thrill is making two holes in one. His former Boston teammate Bruce Hurst idolizes Roger, not just for his pitching ability but for his competitive nature and their friendly battles on golf courses around the country.

When Hurst signed with the San Diego Padres as a free agent in 1988 every day he would tell stories about Roger and the friendly pranks Roger would pull. "He's the best," Hurst said at the time.

"There's no one like him because he's so much fun to be around."

The feeling was mutual. Roger appreciated Hurst's will to win and in 1986, the year the Red Sox won the American League pennant, said that Hurst was "by age, experience and character—the leader of the pitching staff."

As a teammate, Hurst says Roger was there whenever you needed him. The two would often discuss the art of pitching and work on mechanics. Hurst felt so strongly about Roger that one time in 1986 when Roger got in an argument with an umpire at first base, it was Hurst who hustled out of the dugout to defend his teammate and he wound up being ejected. The umpire said Hurst used a profanity. Hurst is a devout Mormon and does not curse. "That is one of the most ridiculous things I've ever heard," Roger said at the time. "He might have said, 'gosh darn.'"

***Roger talks things over with Toronto first baseman
Carlos Delgado. (AP/Wide World Photos)***

The camaraderie of baseball is what makes the game special for Roger and is what makes him such a lover of sports in general. His house is a shrine to sports of all sorts, filled with memorabilia of great athletes. Roger's pride and joy is a Hank Aaron jersey that is signed by all the modern-day 500 home-run hitters and a Nolan Ryan jersey signed by the 300-game winners. He has shelves of autographed baseballs, bats, basketballs and footballs and specially made honeycomb shelves to house his golf ball collection. Roger said so much other athletes were asking him for his autograph, that he decided to start asking for their autographs.

Sports Illustrated writer Gerry Callahan, who lives in Boston and has a radio show there, says that Roger is one of the most unique athletes in the world, not only because of his ability on the mound, but his ability to juggle his life in so many directions. Says Callahan, "People run up to him on the tee for autographs, his cell phone is ringing, and all the while Clemens is talking. In his self-styled Texas lingo he is analyzing each approach, reading each putt and saluting each good shot from everyone in his foursome. He is talking about football, Italian food, his Harley, roller hockey."

Then when his foursome gets backed up, Roger reels off half a dozen jokes to fill the time. Being Roger Clemens may seem like being a full-time job, but the pitcher with the golden arm and golden nonstop voice, has more fun then a teenager at Six Flags. Roger's roller coaster is always going at full speed and Roger has his hands held high in triumph.

Erik Hanson was a pitching-mate of Roger's in both Boston and Toronto and he amazed by both Rogers—the one on the mound and the one on top of the mountain of life, living every moment to its fullest.

"I don't think anyone could have more desire than Roger has every year," Hanson told *SI.* "More than a lot of people, Roger really enjoys who he is. Everyone would like to be as rich and famous as Roger is, but I often wonder how many people could handle it. I don't know if I could. So many people want a piece of Roger, and most of the time he handles it remarkably well."

That desire first came into the public light when Roger won the national championship at the University of Texas in 1983. He was taken by the Mets in the 12th round of the 1981 draft after playing for a year at San Jacinto Junior College in Texas, but elected to transfer to Texas. That turned out to be a great decision because he won a national championship at Texas in 1983, one-year after losing the final championship game on two unearned runs. The free agent draft was held the week Roger won the championship and he was selected in the first

Roger's favorite nickname is "Possessed Rebel." (AP/ Wide World Photos)

round (19th pick overall) by the Red Sox and signed with them for a bonus for $121,000. Four major league pitchers came from that one college team: Clemens, Calvin Schiraldi, Bruce Ruffin and Mike Capel. Eight pitchers from that staff went into professional baseball.

Roger began his professional career pitching for Winter Haven in the Class A Florida State League. It only tool four games for the Red Sox to realize he was ready for a higher level. Roger was 3-1 with a 1.24 ERA, pitching three complete games and striking out 36 batters with no walks in 29 innings. He was promoted to New Britain, Connecticut in the Double A Eastern League and was just as impressive. He finished the year there by going 4-1 with a 1.38 ERA. In 52 innings, he allowed only 31 hits, struck out 59 batters and walked only 12.

Roger began the 1984 season having up again, this time to Red Sox' top farm team, the Pawtucket,

Rhode Island Red Sox in the International League. He pitched in seven games, and even though he had a losing record, 2-3, he had a 1.93 ERA. In 46 2/3 innings, Roger had allowed just 39 hits, struck out 50 and walked only 14 batters. The Red Sox decided he was ready for the major leagues.

Roger won nine games for the Red Sox that year, and won seven more in 1985, learning all time what he needed to do to break through at the major-league level, which he did in Boston's championship season in 1986. While he is known the world over as The Rocket, Roger's favorite nickname is Possessed Rebel. He learned early that any good pitcher could win when he has his best stuff. It's figuring out how to win when things aren't going your way is what makes you successful.

"You've got to use everything you have to win," Roger says. "I tell the young guys you have to go out there and win when things aren't working for you, when everything doesn't feel right. You are not going to have your 'A' game every night, but you have to act like you have it.

"I see some pitchers in the clubhouse before a start and you can tell they're afraid to lose," he says. "I tell them, 'If you don't want them to beat you, they're not going to beat you. It's all up to you.'

Don Zimmer started the 1999 season as Yankee interim manager because Joe Torre was recovering from cancer surgery. On Opening Night against the Oakland A's in Oakland, Zimmer saw something he had never seen his 51 years in professional baseball—The Rocket ready to blast off.

"I have never seen anybody as high to win a game, as Clemens was in the dugout in the first inning," Zimmer says. "He was like a wild lion. When the game started, it looked like he was pitching for a World Series win. That's the way he went about it and that's the way he was rooting for the (Yankee) hitters."

Roger takes a cut during a rare at-bat. (AP/Wide World Photos)

From a young age Roger learned that he was responsible for his own performance. After the death of his stepfather, the Clemens family moved from Mowton, and he excelled in three sports at Spring Woods High School—baseball, football and basketball. He was mature beyond his years.

In that 1983 College World Series, he beat Alabama in the championship game, completing a 25-7 run in his two years at Texas. Ten years later he became the first University of Texas baseball player to have his number (21) retired. Success did not come easy.

The Workhorse

Early in the morning, when the dew is still on the grass, you can find Roger hard at work. Hours before his teammates arrive at spring training, Roger will be running, three or four miles. He'll do 200 push-ups and 200 sit-ups and other exercises. Then he'll go to work. "A lot of people have athletic ability," his old Boston pitching coach Bill Fischer once said, "but very few make use of every ounce of it the way he does."

Roger approaches baseball with a football mentality. And he loves to prove people wrong. There is

Roger is always trying to bring out the best in himself.
(AP/Wide World Photos)

always another challenge in front of him. With the Yankees, it's the fact that his overall post-season record is 1-2 with a 3.88 ERA. The man he replaced, David Wells, was 8-1 in the post-season with a 2.74 ERA. He is so into the game that on the mound he has had to wear a customized mouth guard to protect his teeth from constant grinding. Off the field he drives a Harley Davidson motorcycle and knows how to have fun, but when he crosses the white lines of first and third base Roger is all business.

And in control, his thinking is simple. He's in charge. He has the ball in his hands. "All they do is tell pitchers what not to throw hitters," he once said of his attack mentality. "But it's the defense that is the offense in baseball. The pitcher has the ball and what the hitter does is predicated on what the pitcher does, not vice-versa."

He combines hard work with the high expectations. "I've had some kind of work schedule since high school," he says. "I remember being a sophomore. Some of the kids would have nice cars. I would run back and forth the two miles to school. I haven't lost sight of where it's got me. When you do accomplish good things, it makes it easier to get up and do the work."

Roger is one of those special people that bring out the best in everyone else because he's always trying to bring out the best in himself. You not only admire his work ethic, you want to try to copy him. The same is true for teammates of Michael Jordan. Be Like Mike is more than a saying. Teammates want to Be Like Roger, too. His competitive spirit is amazing. His message is simple: No matter what you do, try to do your best or you're cheating yourself.

Yankee right fielder Paul O'Neill has a similar type of serious game-face as Roger. He says facing Clemens pumps you up as an opponent. "He just has an aura around him," O'Neill explains. "When you know you are going to face him, you run for an extra 10 minutes, try to grab some more time in the batting cage that day."

Considering that opposing hitters always get geared up for Roger makes his success even that much more incredible. Roger's competitive spirit has driven him to become the only pitcher to win five Cy Young Awards (1986, 1987, 1991, 1997, 1998). It enabled him to strike out 20 batters in a game twice. That was why he pitched a one-hitter against the Indians on September 10, 1988, his low-hit game of his career, and how he won 20 straight games from June 3, 1998 until June 6, 1999. It is why he went into the 1999 season with a career

Roger has five 20-win seasons. (AP/Wide World Photos)

233-124 record and a lifetime ERA of 2.95. Five times he has won 20 games. Three times he has won 18 games.

When he was a mere mortal of a pitcher in 1995 and 1996, he made the decision to move on to Toronto. Like always, he had something to prove. "I knew I could still pitch," he says. "The way people were talking about it was like I should have been throwing out the ceremonial first pitch."

His two years in Toronto, Roger led the American League in wins, ERA and strikeouts (271) becoming only the fourth pitcher in the history of baseball to accomplish the feat, something that happens about once every 30 years. Only Hall of Famers Grover Cleveland Alexander (1915-16), Lefty Grove (1930-31) and Sandy Koufax (1965-66) had done it before. In 1998, opponents only batted .198 against him. He finished the season with a 15-game winning streak.

For Roger, momentous moments are every-where you look. When he struck out Tampa Bay's Randy Win on July 5, 1998 he became just the 11th pitcher in major league history to register 3,000 career strikeouts and on September 16th of that year, moved into 10th place on the all-time strikeout list ahead of Bob Gibson. He finished that season with 3,153 career strikeouts. He averaged 273 strikeouts from 1996-98. If he pitches four more years at that pace he will have 4,246 strikeouts. Only Nolan Ryan (5,714) will have more in the history of the game.

Six times Roger has won the ERA title, which means he gave up the fewest amount of earned runs in the league. Only Lefty Grove (9) has won more ERA titles. He finished the 1998 season with a 20-7 mark, a 2.27 ERA and 263 strikeouts. In his two seasons in Toronto he had struck out 555 batters, more batters than he ever struck out in back-to-back seasons. At the age of 36, the Rocket's Red Glare is still glowing, the glare opposing hitters never forget when they step into the batter's box.

And there is still plenty of pitching to be done. For there was still one goal that had eluded him his entire 14-year major league career—winning a championship.

Roger entered the 1999 season with a 2.95 ERA. (AP/ Wide World Photos)

The Quest for the Ring

When Roger signed with the Blue Jays, leaving Boston behind, he did it with the hopes of finally winning the championship that he came so close to in 1986. "Roger is a North American icon," Paul Beeston said at the time. "He's had a Hall of Fame career but no ring."

Signing with the New York Yankees can make that championship dream finally come true. Yankee owner George Steinbrenner has learned that it is not the most talented team that wins champion-

Roger's wife, Debbie, says he "has a strong inner drive to win." (AP/Wide World Photos)

ships, but the team with the most talent and the hunger to win. By trading for Clemens he has assured himself that the pitching staff will be self-motivated with the likes of Roger and David Cone.

Paul Quantrill, an old teammate says of Roger, "I think he'd trade all his Cy Youngs for another shot in the World Series."

Baseball can be the simplest game. It usually comes down to pitching and the Yankees have plenty of that. Still, consider this: Roger's five Cy Young Awards are one more than the Yankees have won as a team since the award was started in 1956. His wife Debbie explained his will to win once to the *Boston Globe*. "Roger has a strong inner drive to win," she said. "Not just in baseball. But in life. He thinks of winning on all levels as a completion, as if he has come full circle. He is not just interested in doing his best."

Winning at everything and anything. During his first spring training with the Yankees, Roger, with 16 years of major league experience under his belt, relentlessly pushed himself like a rookie. He was not only to set an example for his new teammates, but also to put himself at the top of his game with his new team. He cared just as much about running wind sprints and winning those races as he does about a World Series game. Year-to-year games change, situations change, but the fire is always the same.

As Roger crosses the finish line in those sprints, he pumps a fist in triumph. Beating players more than 10 years younger than him means something. It is the success of giving your best. Roger even tried to influence Yankee pitcher Hideki Irabu by showing the Japanese pitcher how hard he works. Roger's Way is one way—full speed ahead. Says Yankee reliever Jeff Nelson of the sprints, "No one thinks those sprints are races, except for Roger."

It is that type of competitiveness that feeds Roger's spirit, keeps him strong and rises those around him to a new level. George Steinbrenner knew just what he was doing when he added Roger to his roster of hard-working stars that had won two World Championships in three years. "I was worried about complacency," Steinbrenner says.

David Cone, like Roger, is a veteran pitcher driven to win. It is those kind of players that keep a major league clubhouse hungry and pointed in the right direction. Baseball is a game, but it takes a combination of talent and desire to win. Ballplayers call that a professional attitude. That's what Roger brings to the clubhouse every day. "He can't help but lead," Cone said, "because guys are going to watch everything he does and follow him."

Everyone is watching. When Roger first took the mound as a Yankee in an exhibition game there were 17 photographers taking the picture of his first pinstriped pitch. *Sports Illustrated* called Roger the Yankees' Booster Rocket because he is just what the team needs to win another title. *New York Post* columnist Wallace Matthews said adding Clemens to the Yankees was like adding floors to the Empire State Building—how high can you go?

Roger's longtime friend Mike Capel, who pitched with Roger at the University of Texas, knows that Roger brings the kind of intangibles that a team must have to succeed, not to mention the ability to blow the ball by the hitter. "People see him on the mound and they think he's some kind of superintense maniac," Capel once told *Sports Illustrated*. "But when he's not playing, he's a different person. He just wants to enjoy life. He's a big teddy bear and he'll do anything for anybody."

That's the kind of athlete New York embraces. This is a city that loves its heroes to be real people as well as real stars. "I'm pretty jacked up for every start," he said after his first start as a Yankee. "Taking the field with these guys is very special. I was able to channel my emotions. I was happy with that." Still, no matter how perfect he is on the mound, Roger admits, "You're never satisfied." He always wants to do better. That is the secret to his success.

Capel went on to tell such a story about the Real Roger. In August of 1996 Capel's father had to be taken off life support in a Houston-area hospital. Who showed up unannounced and spent the night with the grieving Capel? Roger did. A friend was in need. Roger put the difficult situation in perspective for his friend Mike, telling him, "Be thankful for the time you had with your dad."

When Roger finally wins that championship ring, you can be sure there will be tears of joy in his eyes and he will think back to that night in Ohio when his stepfather passed away. This will be a championship not only for his step-dad, but also for his own children, a championship for generations, not just for Roger.

"I just want to get my hands on one of those banners," he told the New York sportswriters in spring training. "You can't be afraid to go for it."

On that night long ago young Roger did not just climb a wobbly stack of books to peer out a window to see the real world, a view that put his own life in perspective at such an early age. Those were the first difficult steps he took to climb the mountain of success.

Roger Clemens Quick Facts

Full Name: Roger Clemens

Team: New York Yankees

Hometown: Dayton, OH

Resides: Houston, TX

Position: Pitcher

Jersey Number: 12

Bats: Right

Throws: Right

Height: 6' 4"

Weight: 230

Birthdate: August 4, 1962

1998 Highlight: Won record fifth Cy Young Award, his second in a row.

Roger Clemens' Career Record

Year	Club	W-L	ERA	G	GS	CG	ShO	IP	H	R	ER	BB	SO
1983	Winter Haven	3-1	1.24	4	4	3	1	29.0	22	4	4	62	36
	New Britain	4-1	1.38	7	7	1	1	52.0	31	8	8	12	59
1984	Pawtucket	2-3	1.93	7	6	3	1	46.2	39	12	10	14	50
	Boston	9-4	4.32	21	20	5	1	133.1	146	67	64	29	126
1985	Boston	7-5	3.29	15	15	3	1	98.1	83	38	36	37	74
1986	Boston	24-4	2.48	33	33	10	1	254.0	179	77	70	67	238
1987	Boston	20-9	2.97	36	36	18	7	281.2	248	100	93	83	256
1988	Boston	18-12	2.93	35	35	14	8	264.0	217	93	86	62	291
1989	Boston	17-11	3.13	35	35	8	3	253.1	215	101	88	93	230
1990	Boston	21-6	1.93	31	31	7	4	228.1	193	59	49	54	209
1991	Boston	18-10	2.62	35	35	13	4	271.1	219	93	79	65	241
1992	Boston	18-11	2.41	32	32	11	5	246.2	203	80	66	62	208
1993	Boston	11-14	4.46	29	29	2	1	191.2	170	99	95	67	160
1994	Boston	9-7	2.85	24	24	3	1	170.2	124	62	54	71	168
1995	Boston	10-5	4.18	23	23	0	0	140.0	141	70	65	60	132
1996	Boston	10-13	3.63	34	34	6	2	242.2	216	106	98	106	257

Year	Club	W-L	ERA	G	GS	CG	ShO	IP	H	R	ER	BB	SO
1997	Toronto	21-7	2.05	34	34	9	3	264.0	204	65	60	68	292
1998	Toronto	20-6	2.65	33	33	5	3	234.2	169	78	69	88	271
M.L. TOTALS		233-124	2.95	450	449	114	44	3274.2	2732	1188	1072	1012	3153

1998 Game by Game

Date	Opp	W/L	IP	H	R	ER	HR	BB	SO
Apr. 1	Min	W	7.0	2	1	1	0	3	3
Apr. 7	@Min	L	0.0	0	2	2	0	2	0
Apr. 17	ChA	W	6.2	5	1	1	0	2	7
Apr. 22	NYA	L	6.2	7	9	6	0	4	6
Apr. 27	@NYA	L	7.0	3	1	1	0	6	8
May 2	@Oak	W	7.0	1	0	0	0	2	7
May 7	@Sea	W	7.0	7	0	0	0	3	6
May 13	Oak	L	8.0	4	4	1	0	6	9

Roger won three Cy Young Awards in Boston. (AP/Wide World Photos)

Date	Opp	W/L	IP	H	R	ER	HR	BB	SO
May 18	Sea	L	5.0	10	9	9	1	3	5
May 23	@Cle	W	8.0	3	2	2	1	3	9
May 29	Cle	L	7.0	7	4	4	1	4	9
June 3	Det	W	9.0**	4	1	1	0	0	10
June 8	@Fla	—	7.0	7	3	3	0	3	8
June 14	Bal	W	5.1	6	4	4	0	5	3
June 19	@Bal	—	5.0	7	4	3	2	4	8
June 24	@Mon	W	7.0	12	5	5	1	1	4
June 30	NYN	W	9.0**	6	3	3	1	1	11
July 5	TBay	—	7.1	5	1	1	0	4	7
July 12	@Det	W	7.1	5	2	2	1	3	10
July 17	NYA	W	7.0	5	1	1	0	2	10
July 22	ChA	W	8.0	3	0	0	0	2	4
July 28	Tex	W	6.2	7	3	3	0	2	4
Aug. 2	@Min	W	8.0	6	2	1	0	1	14

Date	Opp	W/L	IP	H	R	ER	HR	BB	SO
Aug. 9	Oak	—	7.0	5	3	2	0	3	8
Aug. 15	Ana	—	8.0	6	2	2	0	1	15
Aug. 20	@Sea	W*	9.0**	3	0	0	0	2	6
Aug. 25	Kan Ci	W*	9.0**	3	0	0	0	0	18
Aug. 30	Min	W*	9.0**	2	0	0	0	3	7
Sep. 5	Bos	W	8.0	3	2	2	0	3	11
Sep. 11	@NYA	—	5.0	7	3	3	0	1	7
Sep. 16	@Det	W	7.2	4	1	1	1	4	11
Sep. 21	Bal	W	8.0	7	1	1	0	3	15
Sep. 26	Det	—	8.0	7	4	4	2	2	11

* Shut-out

** Complete Game

1998 American League Cy Young Award Voting

Roger Clemens, Tor	140.0
Pedro Martinez, Bos	65.0
David Wells, Yankees	31.0
David Cone, Yankees	16.0

1997 American League Cy Young Award Voting

Roger Clemens, Tor	134.0
Randy Johnson, Sea	77.0
Brad Radke, Min	17.0
Randy Myers, Bal	14.0
Andy Pettitte, Yankees	9.0
Mike Mussina, Bal	1.0

Roger has only had one losing season in the majors.
(AP/Wide World Photos)

1991 American League Cy Young Award Voting

Roger Clemens, Bos	119.0
Scott Erickson, Min	56.0
Jim Abbott, Cal	26.0
Jack Morris, Min	17.0
Bryan Harvey, Cal	10.0
Mark Langston, Cal	7.0
Kevin Tapani, Min	6.0
Bill Gullickson, Det	5.0
Jack McDowell, White Sox	3.0
Duane Ward, Tor	3.0

1987 American League Cy Young Award Voting

Roger Clemens, Bos	124.0
Jimmy Key, Tor	64.0
Dave Stewart, Oak	32.0
Doyle Alexander, Det	8.0
Mark Langston, Sea	7.0
Teddy Higuera, Mil	5.0
Frank Viola, Min	5.0
Jeff Reardon, Min	4.0
Jack Morris, Det	3.0

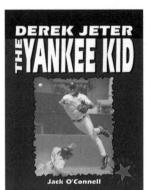

Derek Jeter:
The Yankee Kid
Author: Jack O'Connell
ISBN: 1-58261-043-6

In 1996 Derek burst onto the scene as one of the most promising young shortstops to hit the big leagues in a long time. His hitting prowess and ability to turn the double play have definitely fulfilled the early predictions of greatness.

A native of Kalamazoo, MI, Jeter has remained well grounded. He patiently signs autographs and takes time to talk to the young fans who will be eager to read more about him in this book.

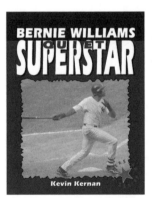

Bernie Williams:
Quiet Superstar
Author: Kevin Kernan
ISBN: 1-58261-044-4

Bernie Williams, a guitar-strumming native of Puerto Rico, is not only popular with his teammates, but is considered by top team officials to be the heir to DiMaggio and Mantle fame.

He draws frequent comparisons to Roberto Clemente, perhaps the greatest player ever from Puerto Rico. Like Clemente, Williams is humble, unassuming, and carries himself with quiet dignity. Also like Clemente, he plays with rare determination and a special elegance. He's married, and serves as a role model not only for his three children, but for his young fans here and in Puerto Rico.

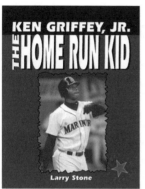
Larry Stone

Ken Griffey, Jr.: The Home Run Kid

Author: Larry Stone
ISBN: 1-58261-041-x

Capable of hitting majestic home runs, making breathtaking catches, and speeding around the bases to beat the tag by a split second, Ken Griffey, Jr. is baseball's Michael Jordan. Amazingly, Ken reached the Major Leagues at age 19, made his first All-Star team at 20, and produced his first 100 RBI season at 21.

The son of Ken Griffey, Sr., Ken is part of the only father-son combination to play in the same outfield together in the same game, and, like Barry Bonds, he's a famous son who turned out to be a better player than his father.

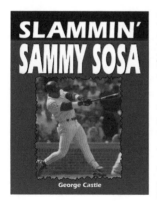
George Castle

Sammy Sosa: Slammin' Sammy

Author: George Castle
ISBN: 1-58261-029-0

1998 was a break-out year for Sammy as he amassed 66 home runs, led the Chicago Cubs into the playoffs and finished the year with baseball's ultimate individual honor, MVP.

When the national spotlight was shone on Sammy during his home run chase with Mark McGwire, America got to see what a special person he is. His infectious good humor and kind heart have made him a role model across the country.

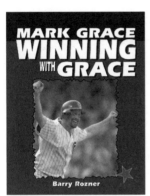

Mark Grace: Winning with Grace

Author: Barry Rozner
ISBN: 1-58261-056-8

This southern California native and San Diego State alumnus has been playing baseball in the windy city for nearly fifteen years. Apparently the cold hasn't affected his game. Mark is an all-around player who can hit to all fields and play great defense.

Mark's outgoing personality has allowed him to evolve into one of Chicago's favorite sons. He is also community minded and some of his favorite charities include the Leukemia Society of America and Easter Seals.

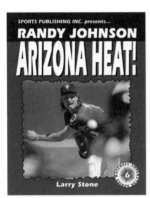

Randy Johnson: Arizona Heat!

Author: Larry Stone
ISBN: 1-58261-042-8

One of the hardest throwing pitchers in the Major Leagues, and, at 6'10" the tallest, the towering figure of Randy Johnson on the mound is an imposing sight which strikes fear into the hearts of even the most determined opposing batters.

Perhaps the most amazing thing about Randy is his consistency in recording strikeouts. He is one of only four pitchers to lead the league in strikeouts for four consecutive seasons. With his recent signing with the Diamondbacks, his career has been rejuvenated and he shows no signs of slowing down.

Omar Vizquel: The Man with the Golden Glove

Author: Dennis Manoloff
ISBN: 1-58261-045-2

Omar has a career fielding percentage of .982 which is the highest career fielding percentage for any shortstop with at least 1,000 games played.

Omar is a long way from his hometown of Caracas, Venezuela, but his talents as a shortstop put him at an even greater distance from his peers while he is on the field.

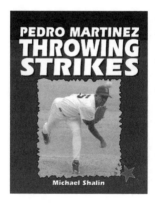

Pedro Martinez: Throwing Strikes

Author: Mike Shalin
ISBN: 1-58261-047-9

The 1997 National League Cy Young Award winner is always teased because of his boyish looks. He's sometimes mistaken for the batboy, but his curve ball and slider leave little doubt that he's one of the premier pitchers in the American League.

It is fitting that Martinez is pitching in Boston, where the passion for baseball runs as high as it does in his native Dominican Republic.

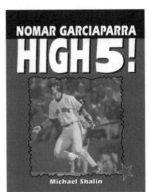

Nomar Garciaparra: High 5!

Author: Mike Shalin
ISBN: 1-58261-053-3

An All-American at Georgia Tech, a star on the 1992 U.S. Olympic Team, the twelfth overall pick in the 1994 draft, and the 1997 American League Rookie of the Year, Garciaparra has exemplified excellence on every level.

At shortstop, he'll glide deep into the hole, stab a sharply hit grounder, then throw out an opponent on the run. At the plate, he'll uncoil his body and deliver a clutch double or game-winning homer. Nomar is one of the game's most complete players.

Juan Gonzalez: Juan Gone!

Author: Evan Grant
ISBN: 1-58261-048-7

One of the most prodigious and feared sluggers in the major leagues, Gonzalez was a two-time home run king by the time he was 24 years old.

After having something of a personal crisis in 1996, the Puerto Rican redirected his priorities and now says baseball is the third most important thing in his life after God and family.

♣

Mo Vaughn:
Angel on a Mission
Author: Mike Shalin
ISBN: 1-58261-046-0

Growing up in Connecticut, this Angels slugger learned the difference between right and wrong and the value of honesty and integrity from his parents early on, lessons that have stayed with him his whole life.

This former American League MVP was so active in Boston charities and youth programs that he quickly became one of the most popular players ever to don the Red Sox uniform.

Mo will be a welcome addition to the Angels line-up and the Anaheim community.

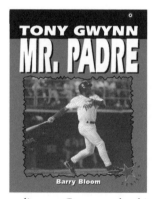

Tony Gwynn:
Mr. Padre
Author: Barry Bloom
ISBN: 1-58261-049-5

Tony is regarded as one of the greatest hitters of all-time. He is one of only three hitters in baseball history to win eight batting titles (the others: Ty Cobb and Honus Wagner).

In 1995 he won the Branch Rickey Award for Community Service by a major leaguer. He is unfailingly humble and always accessible, and he holds the game in deep respect. A throwback to an earlier era, Gwynn makes hitting look effortless, but no one works harder at his craft.

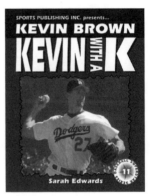

Kevin Brown:
That's Kevin with a "K"
Author: Jacqueline Salman
ISBN: 1-58261-050-9

Kevin was born in McIntyre, Georgia and played college baseball for Georgia Tech. Since then he has become one of baseball's most dominant pitchers and when on top of his game, he is virtually unhittable.

Kevin transformed the Florida Marlins and San Diego Padres into World Series contenders in consecutive seasons, and now he takes his winning attitude and talent to the Los Angeles Dodgers.

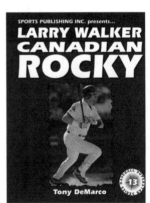

Larry Walker:
Canadian Rocky
Author: Tony DeMarco
ISBN: 1-58261-052-5

Growing up in Canada, Larry had his sights set on being a hockey player. He was a skater, not a slugger, but when a junior league hockey coach left him off the team in favor of his nephew, it was hockey's loss and baseball's gain.

Although the Rockies' star is known mostly for his hitting, he has won three Gold Glove awards, and has worked hard to turn himself into a complete, all-around ballplayer. Larry became the first Canadian to win the MVP award.

SUPERSTAR SERIES

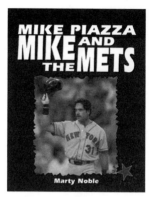

Mike Piazza:
Mike and the Mets
Author: Marty Noble
ISBN: 1-58261-051-7

A total of 1,389 players were selected ahead of Mike Piazza in the 1988 draft, who wasn't picked until the 62nd round, and then only because Tommy Lasorda urged the Dodgers to take him as a favor to his friend Vince Piazza, Mike's father.

Named in the same breath with great catchers of another era like Bench, Dickey and Berra, Mike has proved the validity of his father's constant reminder "If you work hard, dreams do come true."

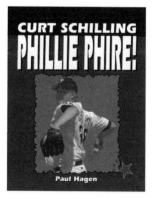

Curt Schilling:
Phillie Phire!
Author: Paul Hagen
ISBN: 1-58261-055-x

Born in Anchorage, Alaska, Schilling has found a warm reception from the Philadelphia Phillies faithful. He has amassed 300+ strikeouts in the past two seasons and even holds the National League record for most strikeouts by a right handed pitcher at 319.

This book tells of the difficulties Curt faced being traded several times as a young player, and how he has been able to deal with off-the-field problems.

Mark McGwire: Mac Attack!

Author: Rob Rains
ISBN: 1-58261-004-5

Mac Attack! describes how McGwire overcame poor eyesight and various injuries to become one of the most revered hitters in baseball today. He quickly has become a legendary figure in St. Louis, the home to baseball legends such as Stan Musial, Lou Brock, Bob Gibson, Red Schoendienst and Ozzie Smith. McGwire thought about being a police officer growing up, but he hit a home run in his first Little League at-bat and the rest is history.

Roger Clemens: Rocket!

Author: Kevin Kernan
ISBN: 1-58261-128-9

When it comes to dominance, few pitchers in baseball history compare to Yankees' fireballer Roger Clemens. Kevin Kernan offers this look at Clemens, and how all of his individual achievements would have so much more meaning with a World Series Ring.

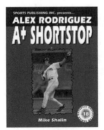

Alex Rodriguez: A+ Shortstop

ISBN: 1-58261-104-1

A-Rod has turned himself into one of the most electrifying players in baseball. This look at the Mariners' All-Star details his success, including his American League record in 1998 of 42 home runs for a shortstop, and his membership in the exclusive 40-40 club.

Baseball
SuperStar Series Titles

Collect Them All!

_____ Kevin Brown: Kevin with a "K"

_____ Roger Clemens: Rocket!

_____ Juan Gonzalez: Juan Gone!

_____ Mark Grace: Winning With Grace

_____ Ken Griffey, Jr.: The Home Run Kid

_____ Tony Gwynn: Mr. Padre

_____ Derek Jeter: The Yankee Kid

_____ Randy Johnson: Arizona Heat!

_____ Pedro Martinez: Throwing Strikes

_____ Mike Piazza: Mike and the Mets

_____ Alex Rodriguez: A+ Shortstop

_____ Curt Schilling: Philly Phire!

_____ Sammy Sosa: Slammin' Sammy

_____ Mo Vaughn: Angel on a Mission

Omar Vizquel:
_____ The Man with a Golden Glove

_____ Larry Walker: Canadian Rocky

_____ Bernie Williams: Quiet Superstar

_____ Mark McGwire: Mac Attack!

Available by calling 877-424-BOOK